How People Lived in America
Going to School in American History

by Dana Meachen Rau

Reading consultant:
Susan Nations, M.Ed.,
author/literacy coach/
consultant in literacy development

Please visit our web site at: **www.garethstevens.com**
**For a free color catalog describing Weekly Reader® Early Learning Library's list
of high-quality books, call 1-877-445-5824 (USA) or 1-800-387-3178 (Canada).
Weekly Reader® Early Learning Library's fax: (414) 336-0164.**

Library of Congress Cataloging-in-Publication Data

Rau, Dana Meachen, 1971-
    Going to school in American history / by Dana Meachen Rau.
      p. cm. — (How people lived in America)
    Includes bibliographical references and index.
    ISBN-10: 0-8368-7207-X — ISBN-13: 978-0-8368-7207-1 (lib. bdg.)
    ISBN-10: 0-8368-7214-2 — ISBN-13: 978-0-8368-7214-9 (softcover)
    1. Education—United States—History—Juvenile literature. I. Title.
  LA205.R38   2007
  370.973'09—dc22   2006008635

This edition first published in 2007 by
Weekly Reader® Early Learning Library
A Member of the WRC Media Family of Companies
330 West Olive Street, Suite 100
Milwaukee, WI 53212 USA

Editor: Barbara Kiely Miller
Art direction: Tammy West
Cover design and page layout: Kami Strunsee
Picture research: Sabrina Crewe

Picture credits: Cover, title page © CORBIS; p. 4 © Ariel Skelley/CORBIS; pp. 6, 7, 8, 9, 11,
13, 16, 17, 19 The Granger Collection, New York; pp. 10, 15, 20 Library of Congress; pp. 12,
21 © Bettmann/CORBIS; pp. 14, 18 © North Wind Picture Archives

Printed in the United States of America

1 2 3 4 5 6 7 8 9 10 09 08 07 06

Table of Contents

Cover: At this country school, some children were so poor that they did not have shoes.

Teachers and computers help students learn at school.

Going to School Today

Today, busy children work at **computers** in their classrooms. All children have a chance to go to school now. But long ago, some people were not allowed in a classroom. Poor children, girls, and African Americans were sometimes told they could not go to school.

Long ago, schools in America . . .

- did not have computers;
- did not have chalkboards or whiteboards;
- did not have crayons, markers, pencils, or even paper;
- did not have desks;
- did not have school buses;
- did not have libraries filled with books;
- did not have colorful classrooms;
- did not have heat in winter;
- did not have books to learn from.

The children of settlers worked at home all day.

Early American Schools

In the early 1600s, America did not have any schools. Children spent the day doing **chores**, or jobs, at home. Boys helped their fathers build barns. They hunted for food together. Girls helped their mothers cook and sew.

At the end of a busy day, parents taught their children to read and write at home. They read together from their family's Bible. More people came to live in America. Villages and towns started to grow. In the middle of the 1600s, towns started to build schools.

Many settlers learned to read from a Bible.

All the children who lived near a town went to the same one-room school. Some schools were very crowded.

Most of America's first schools had only one room. Children sat on wooden benches. A fireplace kept the students warm in winter. One teacher taught children of all ages. The teacher taught them to read, write, and do math.

Early schools did not have much paper. Children wrote on bark from birch trees or on small chalkboards called **slates**. Children learned to read from a **hornbook**. A hornbook was a wooden paddle with one sheet of paper stuck to it. The hornbook showed the alphabet and a prayer for children to learn.

A thin layer of cow's horn held the paper in place on a hornbook. The horn gave these early books their name.

He that ne'er learns his A, B,
For ever will a Blockhead be ; but he that learns thefe Letters fair,
hall have a Coach to take the Air.

a Apple	b Ball	c C...	n Nag	o Owl	p Peacock
Dog	e Egg	f Fri...	q Queen	r Robin	f Squ rel
g Goat	h Hog	j Judg	t Top	v Vine	w Whale
k King	l Lion	m Mou	Xerxes	young Lamb	z Zani

A Little Child's Prayer.
I Pray God to blefs my Father and Mother, Brothers and Sifters, and all my good Friends. Amen.

Lucy. Wadsworth.
Her Book P o o

This primer is from 1779. It belonged to a young girl who used it to learn the alphabet.

In the 1700s, schools had more paper. Children wrote their lessons with a pen made from a long, stiff feather. They dipped the hard tip of these **quill pens** in ink before writing. Children read from books called **primers**. The primers had simple poems in them.

Boys who were apprentices to a potter learned how to make pots.

Some boys learned how to do a job by becoming **apprentices**. If a boy wanted to be a **carpenter**, he went to live with one. The carpenter taught the boy how to do his job. Boys also became apprentices to barrel makers, shoemakers, and **blacksmiths**.

In some jobs, children's small hands made them good workers.

Not Everyone Gets to Learn

In the early 1800s, most children in America did not go to
school. Some areas did not have schools. Many schools
cost money to go to. Rich people could send their children
to the best schools. Some schools were free. But many
children from poor families could not go to them, either.
They had to work to help their families make money.

Girls went to school only until about the sixth grade. Many people thought it was more important for girls to stay home to learn to cook and sew. But boys went to school until eighth grade. Then boys had choices. They might go to a school for older boys and then on to **college**.

Children played in the schoolyard when classes were done.

Many slave children had to work hard picking cotton. They could not go to school.

Most African Americans worked as **slaves** for white farmers. They had no freedom. Some laws said slaves could not go to school. Slavery ended after the Civil War. But in many places, African American children were still not allowed to go to the same schools as white children.

Lots of Changes

In the 1800s, people wanted more chances for everyone to learn. Thousands of people moved to the United States from other countries. These people are called **immigrants**. They thought schools could teach them how to live and work in America.

These immigrant girls learned how to knit at a class in New York.

At this school for the deaf,
children learned new words
from their teacher.

Women wanted the chance to go to college, just as men did. The first college for women in the country opened in 1821. Some men's colleges started to let women in, too. More schools and colleges for black people opened. Schools for children who could not see or hear were started, too.

In the middle and late 1800s, many children still went to one-room schoolhouses. Schools in larger towns and cities had more rooms and teachers. Many schools were improved. Schools put large chalkboards on their classroom walls. Many states passed laws that said children between the ages of eight and fourteen must go to school.

These students studied how water turns to steam. Some children wrote notes on the chalkboard that the others copied.

This kindergarten class played a game called "the windmill."

Larger schools separated children into different grades and classrooms. Children learned by copying from books and repeating what their teachers said. Some people thought school should be more fun. In 1856, young children began going to **kindergarten**. They learned through playing, songs, and games. Older students went to high schools. These schools added classes in science, history, music, and art.

Everyone Can Learn

Throughout history, most children had to walk to school. In the 1900s, some children rode their bikes to school. Then many neighborhoods started to use school buses. Children no longer had to walk so far.

Children who lived far from school rode their bikes instead of walking home.

Until 1954, many black children were not allowed to go to school with white children.

By the middle of the 1900s, schools in the United States had changed in many ways. But black children still could not go to the same schools as white children. Laws said they had to go to separate schools. Separating people who are from different races is called **segregation**.

Both black and white people worked hard to end segregation. They wanted all children to have the same chances to learn. In 1954, the top judges in the country changed the laws. They said that schools had to welcome all students, no matter the color of their skin. Today, all boys and girls can learn together about the world and each other.

Now all children can have fun at school together.

Glossary

apprentices — people learning a skill or a job by working under skilled workers

blacksmiths — people who heat iron and hammer it into objects such as tools

carpenter — a person who builds or repairs wooden objects and buildings

college — a school attended after high school

hornbook — a wooden paddle with a lesson printed on paper for students to read

immigrants — people who come to a new country or region to live

primers — (*prih* mers) books for teaching children to read. Early primers had simple poems and prayers

quill pens — writing tools made from feathers

segregation — the separation of a group of people from the rest of the people in society

slates — small, handheld chalkboards used for writing

slaves — people who are owned by other people and made to work without pay. They are not free.

For More Information

Books

A One-Room School. Historic Communities (series). Bobbie Kalman (Crabtree Publishing Company)

School in Colonial America. Welcome Books (series). Mark Thomas (Children's Press)

The School Is Not White! A True Story of the Civil Rights Movement. Doreen Rappaport (Hyperion Books for Children)

Web Site

Gettysburg College Special Collections: The New England Primer 1805

www.gettysburg.edu/~tshannon/his341/nep1805contents.html

See the pages of the book used by many children in history

Publisher's note to educators and parents: Our editors have carefully reviewed this Web site to ensure that it is suitable for children. Many Web sites change frequently, however, and we cannot guarantee that a site's future contents will continue to meet our high standards of quality and educational value. Be advised that children should be closely supervised whenever they access the Internet.

Index

About the Author

Dana Meachen Rau is the author of more than one hundred and fifty children's books, including nonfiction and books for early readers. She writes about history, science, geography, people, and even toys! She lives with her family in Burlington, Connecticut.